CONTENTS (CONTINUED)

C000179860

Welcome to the amazing world of the Air Fryer made easy!

Air-frying is a simple and healthy way to cook food, using the 'magic' of hot air.

A quick and easy method of cooking which is not just about frying, as you will see from the wide range of recipes in this book.

The air fryer is an invaluable and versatile piece of kitchen equipment enabling you to prepare quick and delicious meals as well as tasty homemade chips, so you get the great flavour of deep frying with a fraction of the fat content.

Although most people buy an air fryer to make great chips it can be used for so much more. This book has been written with lots of recipes to make you get the most out of your air fryer. Recipes that will hopefully inspire you.

As your air fryer needs only a small amount of oil to work its magic, you may use your favourite quality oil such as olive oil.

This book contains a large selection of my recipe creations which have been tried and tested on a range of air fryers to ensure they are successful.

I love experimenting in the kitchen and would encourage you to do the same. You can adapt the recipes by adding or changing ingredients according to your own taste. In this book there are lots of great 'top tips' and ideas to make the recipes your own.

Where possible, I have tried to use basic store cupboard ingredients to make them quick and easy for everyone. If you have other ingredients to hand, please experiment.

Have fun creating!

Appliance Guide IMPORTANT! Please Read.

This book has been based on Air Fryers that are either like a mini oven or have a pull-out basket to place the food in. All recipes in this book can be cooked in a conventional fan oven. However, if you want to cook larger quantities you may need to adjust the cooking time and temperature accordingly.

Please note...

I recommended a temperature range of 170°c to 180°c on a lot of the recipes (but always follow the manufacturer's guidelines as these take priority).

The above temperatures stop the oil burning. Oil turns to a sticky tar over 190°c this then makes it more difficult to clean your machine.

If your air fryer has a food basket, some of the recipes require your food to be placed in an ovenproof dish and placed in the basket during cooking. This can be any dish that is suitable for a conventional oven and grill.

If your Air fryer does not have a food basket but has a non-stick metal or glass pan, then you can place the food directly into it. (Manufacturer's guidelines always take precedence).

Some air fryers require pre-heating. If this is the case with yours, ensure you do this first. All our recipes have been tested without pre-heating. Please adjust the cooking time as necessary if your air fryer needs pre-heating. If not, simply follow the recipe.

Always follow the manufacturer's guidelines. Always place the food in the correct cooking pan or suitable dish in accordance with the manufacturer's instructions. Never leave your appliance unattended.

Follow correct cooking procedures....

✔ When adding dried herbs or seasoning, always ensure you mix them with a liquid, such as oil to prevent them being blow round your air fryer and sticking to the heating element.

✔ All temperatures, times and instructions are given as a guide only and should always be adjusted accordingly at the time of cooking.

✔ Always check that the food has been thoroughly cooked before consumption.

✔ All recipes are provided as a guide only. Always ensure the recipes are compatible with your manufacturer's appliance.

Only use suitable dishes. By this I mean ovenware that is also grill proof such as stoneware, metal, or oven safe glass dishes. I have a saucepan and frying pan set which has removable handles, some of which fit perfectly in my air fryer. I use these because they are non-stick making them easier to clean.

If you are using silicone cupcake cases or a silicone insert for your basket, please follow the manufacturer's instructions.

Dehydrating in the Air Fryer

Dehydrating preserves the nutritional benefits of raw fruits and vegetables. It is also beneficial for preserving food and giving it a longer shelf life.

Your air fryer will need to have a low temperature setting of approximately 45°c to 80°c (machines may vary) and a steam rack or shelf. The food needs to be thinly spread out (so it may need to be cooked in batches).

You will need to dehydrate food for 2 hours for thinly sliced fruits and vegetables.

Whole fruits and vegetables may take longer or follow your user instruction guide. Some air fryers also have dehydration settings.

Dehydrating Fruits and Vegetables

- Whole Red Chillies (halved)
- Whole Cherry Tomatoes (halved)
- Kale leaves
- Thinly sliced Apples
- Cubes or Rings of Pineapple
- Cubes of Mango
- Thinly sliced Oranges
- Halved Apricots

Beef Jerky

Ingredients
250g Thinly Sliced Topside Beef

Marinade
50ml Worcestershire Sauce
50ml Soy Sauce
1 tsp Honey
½ tsp Onion Powder
½ tsp Chilli Flakes (optional, add more or less as required).

Method

1 Mix together all of the marinade ingredients in a bowl.

2 Add the thinly sliced beef to the marinade and stir until beef is well coated.

3 Cover the bowl with cling film and marinate overnight or for at least 3 hours in the fridge.

4 Remove the beef from the marinade and pat dry with kitchen roll.

5 Place beef strips in the air fryer basket in a single layer, with no overlapping.

6 Cook at 80°c for 2 hours, checking to see if dried out every 30 minutes. If required cook for a further 15-20 minutes until ready.

7 When jerky is ready, allow to cool and store in an airtight container.

BBQ Marinade
Great with Chicken, Pork & Vegetables

Marinade

Ingredients

2 tbsp Tomato Ketchup
1 tsp Soy Sauce
1 heaped tsp Dark Brown Sugar
*(muscovado is best but brown
sugar will work)*
1 tbsp Sweet Chilli Sauce
½ Lemon (juiced)
1 tsp Worcestershire Sauce
Salt & Pepper
Scale up as required.

Method

1 Mix together all of the
   ingredients in a bowl.

2 Add your chosen
   Meat/Vegetables.
   Cover with marinade
   and place in the
   refrigerator for 2 hours.

3 Once marinated place in your air fryer
   and cook at 170-180°c for:
   ● Chicken: 15-20 minutes
   ● Pork: 15-20 minutes
   ● Vegetables: 10-15 minutes

Chinese Marinade
Great with Pork, Chicken, Prawns & Vegetables

Ingredients

1 tsp Ginger (grated)
½ Lemon (juiced)
1 tbsp Soy Sauce
1 tbsp Sweet Chilli Sauce
1 tbsp Olive Oil
1 tsp Five Spice (optional)
Salt & Pepper
Scale up as required.

Method

1 Mix together all of the
   ingredients in a bowl.

2 Add your chosen
   Meat/Fish/Vegetables.
   Cover with marinade
   and place in the
   refrigerator for 2 hours.

3 Once marinated place in your air fryer
   and cook at 170-180°c for:
   ● Chicken: 15-20 minutes.
   ● Pork: 15-20 minutes
   ● Fish: 5-8 minutes
   ● Vegetables: 10-15 minutes

Curry Marinade

Great with Chicken, Fish, Pork, Lamb & Vegetables.

Ingredients

1 tsp Curry Powder
1 tsp Sweet Chilli Sauce
1 tsp Mango Chutney
½ Lime (juiced)
1 tsp Soy Sauce
2 tbsp Full Fat Mayonnaise
(you need the oil content to prevent burning)
Salt & Pepper
Scale up as required.

Method

1. Mix together all of the ingredients in a bowl.

2. Add your chosen Meat/Fish/Vegetables. Cover with marinade and place in the refrigerator for 2 hours.

3. Once marinated place in your air fryer and cook at 170-180°c for:
   - Chicken: 15-20 minutes
   - Pork: 15-20 minutes
   - Lamb: 10-15 minutes
   - Fish: 10-15 minutes
   - Vegetables: 10-15 minutes

Jerk Marinade

Great with Pork, Chicken & Vegetables

Ingredients

2 Red Chillies (finely chopped)
2 Garlic Cloves (finely chopped)
1 tsp All Spice Powder
1 tsp Dried Thyme
1 tsp Cumin
1 tsp Oregano
1 tsp Paprika
1 tsp Turmeric
1 tsp Brown Sugar
2 tbsp Soy Sauce
1 tsp Ground Nutmeg
1 tbsp Olive Oil
Scale up as required.

Method

1. Mix together all of the ingredients in a bowl.

2. Add your chosen Meat/Vegetables. Cover with marinade and place in the refrigerator for 2 hours.

3. Once marinaded place in your air fryer and cook at 170-180°c for:
   - Chicken: 15-20 minutes
   - Pork: 15-20 minutes
   - Vegetables: 10-15 minutes

Lemon and Herb Marinade

Great with Lamb, Chicken, Pork, Fish, Seafood & Vegetables

Marinade

Ingredients

½ Lemon (juiced)
1 tsp Mixed herbs
1 tsp Olive Oil
1 tsp Mango Chutney
Salt & Pepper
Scale up as required.

Method

1 Mix together all of the ingredients in a bowl.

2 Add your chosen Meat/Fish/Vegetables. Cover with marinade and place in the refrigerator for 2 hours.

3 Once marinated place in your air fryer and cook at 170-180°c for:
- Lamb: 10-15 minutes
- Chicken: 15-20 minutes
- Pork: 15-20 minutes
- Fish: 10-15 minutes
- Seafood: 8-12 minutes
- Vegetables: 10-15 minutes

Lime and Ginger Marinade

Great with Chicken, Pork, Fish, Seafood & Vegetables

Ingredients

1 Lime (juiced)
1 tsp Ginger (grated)
1 tsp Soy Sauce
½ Garlic Clove (finely chopped)
Salt & Pepper
Scale up as required.

Method

1 Mix together all of the ingredients in a bowl.

2 Add your chosen Meat/Fish/Vegetables. Cover with marinade and place in the refrigerator for 2 hours.

3 Once marinated place in your air fryer and cook for:
- Chicken: 15-20 minutes
- Pork: 15-20 minutes
- Fish: 10-15 minutes
- Seafood: 8-12 minutes
- Vegetables: 10-15 minutes

Add in 1 tsp of chopped red chilli for an extra kick.

Moroccan Marinade

Great with Lamb, Chicken, Pork, & Vegetables.

Ingredients

1 tsp Harissa Paste
½ tsp Cumin
½ tsp Smoked Paprika
½ Lemon (juiced)
1 tbsp Olive Oil
Salt & Pepper
Scale up as required.

Method

1 Mix together all of the ingredients in a bowl.

2 Add your chosen Meat/Vegetables. Cover with marinade and place in the refrigerator for 2 hours.

3 Once marinated place in your air fryer and cook at 170-180°c for:
- Chicken: 15-20 minutes
- Pork: 15-20 minutes
- Lamb: 10-15 minutes
- Vegetables: 10-15 minutes

Peri Peri Marinade

Great with Beef Steak, Chicken, Pork, & Vegetables

Ingredients

1 Hot Chilli (finely chopped)
1 Garlic Clove (finely chopped)
1 tsp Smoked Paprika
1 tsp Mixed Herbs
½ Lemon (juiced)
1 tsp Sweet Chilli Sauce
Salt & Pepper
Scale up as required.

Method

1 Mix together all of the ingredients in a bowl.

2 Add your chosen Meat/Vegetables. Cover with marinade and place in the refrigerator for 2 hours.

3 Once marinated place in your air fryer and cook for:
- Beef Steaks: 10-15 minutes
- Chicken: 15-20 minutes
- Pork: 15-20 minutes
- Vegetables: 10-15 minutes

Air Fryer Sauces

Roasted Garlic Mayonnaise

3 Cloves of Roasted Garlic
3 tbsp Mayonnaise.

Once cooled squeeze the roasted garlic from the skin and stir into mayonnaise.

Roasted Garlic Butter

100g Butter
3 cloves of Roasted Garlic
1 tbsp Fresh Parsley (chopped)

Once cooled squeeze the roasted garlic from the skin and blend into butter (at room temperature). Add chopped parsley and mix well.

Roasted Garlic

Ingredients

1 head of Garlic
1 tsp Olive Oil
Salt & Pepper
Tin Foil

Method

1   Cut the top off the head of the garlic and place on a square piece of tin foil. Bring the foil up and around the garlic. Pour the olive oil on top and season. Close the ends of the foil over the garlic.

2   Cook at 190°c for 16 to 20 minutes. Open the foil very carefully as steam will escape.

Chilli Mayonnaise

1 tsp Chilli Powder
3 tbsp Mayonnaise

Combine chilli powder and mayonnaise (for medium heat). Add more chilli powder as required for an extra kick.

Why not use dehydrated whole red chillies and blend to a powder?

Stilton Sauce

100g Stilton
1 tsp Sweet Pickle
200ml Double Cream
Salt & Pepper

Crumble the Stilton and add sweet pickle and cream. Place into the air fryer in an ovenproof dish for approx. 5 minutes, stir after every minute of cooking time.

Roasted Tomato Pizza Sauce

Place roasted tomatoes into a food processor (or mash with a fork in a bowl). Add in 1 tsp dried basil, 1 tsp oregano, 1 tbsp lemon juice and stir. If you would like a smooth pizza sauce, then pass the sauce through a fine sieve.

Roasted Tomatoes

Ingredients

300g Cherry Tomatoes
1 tbsp of Olive Oil
Salt & Pepper
1 tsp Minced Garlic
1 tbsp Dried Rosemary
Tin Foil

Method

1   Place the tomatoes on a square piece of tin foil. Bring the foil up and around the tomatoes. Pour the olive oil, garlic, rosemary and season. Close the ends of the foil over the tomatoes and make a parcel.

2   Cook at 190°c for 16 to 20 minutes. Open the foil very carefully as steam will escape.

Can also be great as a side to grilled meats.

Starters and Sides

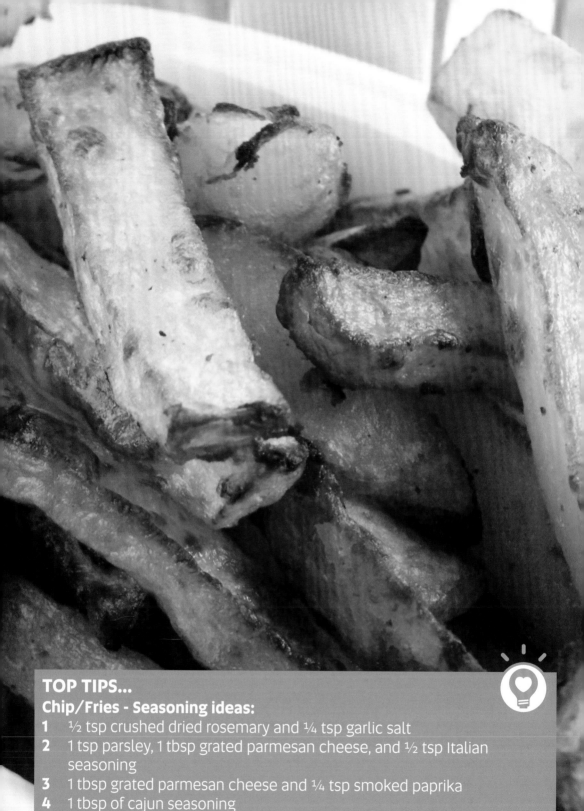

TOP TIPS...
Chip/Fries - Seasoning ideas:

1. ½ tsp crushed dried rosemary and ¼ tsp garlic salt
2. 1 tsp parsley, 1 tbsp grated parmesan cheese, and ½ tsp Italian seasoning
3. 1 tbsp grated parmesan cheese and ¼ tsp smoked paprika
4. 1 tbsp of cajun seasoning
5. Place the chips in a bowl and pour over 1 tsp truffle oil and toss in the bowl. Grate 50g parmesan cheese over the chips and enjoy!

Potato Chips/Fries 🌱
Serves 4

Ingredients
450g Potatoes
(peeled and cut
into ½ inch
sticks)
700ml Water
1 tbsp Olive Oil
Salt & Pepper

Method

1   Put potato sticks in a bowl. Pour in water and let sit for 30 minutes. *(Optional - This helps remove the starch, which makes the potatoes less likely to burn).*

2   Drain the potato sticks, dry in a clean tea towel and place back into a bowl. Drizzle oil over the sticks and season with salt and pepper. Toss to coat evenly.

3   Arrange sticks in a double layer in the fryer basket. Cook at 180°c for 15-20 minutes, tossing every 5 minutes, until golden brown. Sprinkle with salt and desired seasoning.

Sweet Potato Fries 🌱
Serves 2
Ingredients

1 Large Sweet Potato
(peeled and cut into ½ inch sticks)
1 tbsp Olive Oil
½ tsp Paprika
½ tsp Garlic Granules
Salt & Pepper

Method

1   Put sweet potato sticks in a bowl. Drizzle oil over them and season with paprika, garlic, salt and pepper. Toss to coat evenly.

2   Divide sweet potato sticks into 2 or 3 batches for cooking. Place an even layer of sticks in the fry basket and insert in to the air fryer. Cook at 180°c for 10-15 minutes until golden. Repeat with remaining sticks.

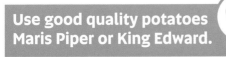
Use good quality potatoes Maris Piper or King Edward.

13

Rapeseed Oil will give the Celeriac a nice golden colour.

For a little kick why not add ¼ tsp curry powder or ¼ Paprika to step 3?

Celeriac Chips 🌿
Serves 4

Ingredients

½ Celeriac Root
(peeled and cut
into ½ inch sticks)
700ml Water
1 tbsp Lemon
Juice
¼ tsp Celery Salt
½ tsp Garlic Granules
½ tsp Mixed Herbs
1 tbsp Oil
Salt & Pepper

Method

1   Put celeriac
    root sticks in a
    bowl. Pour in
    water and
    lime juice. Mix
    and let sit for 20 minutes.

2   Drain the sticks, dry in a clean tea
    towel and place back into the
    bowl.
3   Drizzle oil over the sticks, mix
    together the celery salt, garlic
    granules, mixed herbs, pinch of
    salt & pepper. Sprinkle over sticks
    and toss to coat evenly.
4   Add the sticks to the air fryer
    basket. Cook at 180°c for 25-45
    minutes (depending on thickness)
    checking halfway through, shaking
    the basket every 5 minutes. Cook
    until fries are crisp and browned.

Courgette Curly Fries 🌿
Serves 2
Ingredients

1 Courgette
1 Egg (beaten)
200g Breadcrumbs
100g Grated Parmesan Cheese
1 tbsp of Mixed Herbs
Cooking Spray Oil

Method

1   Cut courgette into batons.
2   Place beaten egg in a shallow
    dish. Combine breadcrumbs,
    parmesan cheese, and mixed
    herbs in a large resealable
    plastic bag. Dip ½ of the
    courgette batons in the beaten
    egg and then place in the bag to
    coat with bread crumb mixture.
3   Spray the basket of the air fryer
    with cooking spray. Arrange
    breaded courgette batons in the
    prepared basket, making sure to
    not overcrowd. Spray the tops
    with cooking spray.
4   Cook at 180°c until crispy (about
    10 minutes), flipping halfway
    through the cooking time.
    Transfer fries to a paper towel-
    lined plate. Repeat breading and
    cooking process with remaining
    courgette batons.

Halloumi Fries 🌿
Serves 2

Ingredients

225g Halloumi
1 tsp Soy Sauce
½ tsp Caster Sugar
½ tsp Mixed Herbs
½ tsp Garlic Granules
1 tsp of Paprika
1 tsp Flour
Pepper
Cooking Spray Oil

Method

1 Cut halloumi into ½ inch sticks.
2 Place the sticks in a shallow dish and coat with soy sauce.
3 Mix together the flour, sugar, garlic, herbs and paprika. Then coat each of the fries with the flour mix.
4 Spray the basket of the air fryer with cooking spray. Arrange sticks in a single layer in the prepared basket making sure to leave space between each. Spray the tops with cooking spray.
5 Cook at 180°c until crispy, about 8-10 minutes, flipping halfway through cook time. Transfer fries to a paper towel-lined plate. Serve immediately. *(Cook in batches if required)*.

Serve with tomato ketchup and sweet chilli sauce.

Roast Potatoes 🌿
Serves 4

Ingredients
450g Maris Piper Potatoes
(peeled and cut into equal size
pieces)
2 Sprigs of Rosemary
1 tsp Yeast Extract
(Marmite/Vegemite-optional)
1 tbsp Oil
1 tbsp Goose Fat or Oil
1 tbsp Hot water

Method

1. Mix together the potatoes and oil in a large bowl.
2. Set the air fryer to 170°c. Pour the potatoes into a suitable dish for your air fryer and cook for 15-25 minutes then remove from air fryer.
3. Mix the yeast extract and goose fat together with 1 tbsp hot water. Pour over the half cooked potatoes and stir. Return potatoes to air fryer and cook for a further 15-20 minutes until golden brown.
4. Add the sprigs of Rosemary and cook for a further 2 minutes, then serve.

Garlic Baby Potatoes 🌿
Serves 4
Ingredients

450g Baby/New Potatoes
(cut into equal pieces)
2 tbsp Olive Oil
2 Garlic Cloves (finely chopped)
½ tsp Lemon Zest
Pinch of Salt

Method

1. Mix together the potatoes, oil and garlic in a large bowl.
2. Arrange potatoes in a single layer in the fryer basket (cook in batches if required). Cook at 180°c for 15-20 minutes until golden brown. Sprinkle with salt and lemon zest before serving.

The smaller you cut the potatoes, the quicker they will cook.

Potato Wedges 🌿
Serves 4

Ingredients

2 Large
Potatoes
(peeled and
cut into
wedges)
1 tbsp Mango
Chutney
½ tsp Garlic
Granules
½ tsp Paprika
1 tbsp Mayonnaise

Dip

50ml Sour Cream
1 tsp Chives (chopped)

Method

1   Place the potato wedges into a large bowl, add the paprika, garlic, mango chutney and mayonnaise. Stir well to coat all wedges.
2   Spray the air fryer basket with oil and place the wedges into basket in a single layer (may need to cook in batches). Cook at 170°c, for 10-15 minutes. Turn the wedges and cook for an additional 10-15 minutes until golden brown.
3   Mix together the Sour Cream and Chives for dip.

Add ½ tsp of chilli powder into step 1 to add a kick!

Hasselback Potatoes 🌿

Ingredients

8 Medium
Potatoes (nice
even shape
long and thin
ones are best)
2 tbsp Butter
Parmesan
Cheese
Breadcrumbs
Paprika
Salt & Pepper

Method

1   Rinse and scrub the potatoes thoroughly.
2   Place the handles of two wooden spoons either side of the potatoes and slice until the knife reaches the spoon handle. This prevents you cutting all the way through. Do this at 5mm intervals all the way along the potatoes.
3   If you are doing these in advance place them in cold water until you are ready to cook as this will stop them tarnishing and turning black.
4   Melt the butter and season with the salt and pepper.
5   Once you are ready to cook make sure they are nice and dry. Brush with the melted, seasoned butter. Try and get it right into the cuts you have made.
6   Place on a suitable tray for an air fryer and cook at 180°c for 30 minutes or until cooked (*times will depend on the size of your potatoes*). Brush with butter every 10 minutes.
7   Mix the breadcrumbs, parmesan and paprika together and sprinkle over the potatoes, cook for a further 5 minutes until golden brown.

> Why not add some finely chopped garlic to your butter for a tasty treat?

Feel free to vary this recipe with any root vegetables that you have or remove any you dislike.

TOP TIPS AND ALTERNATIVES...
A great accompaniment to roast or grilled meat.
Why not add in 1 tsp of ground cumin to step 4,
it would be great with a curry?
Alternatively, Balsamic glaze also works really well.

Roasted Mediterranean Vegetables 🌿
Serves 4

Ingredients

1 Red Pepper (cubed)
1 Yellow Pepper (cubed)
1 Green Pepper (cubed)
½ Aubergine (cubed)
1 Red Onion (cubed)
12 Cherry Tomatoes
1 tsp Tomato Puree
2 Garlic Cloves (finely chopped)
2 tbsp Olive Oil
¼ Tsp dried Mixed Herbs

Method

1   Mix together the peppers, aubergine, onion and 1 tbsp of olive oil in a bowl. Place into an ovenproof deep dish that is suitable for your air fryer.
2   Set the air fryer to 170°c (*if applicable)* and cook for 15 minutes. Remove from air fryer.
3   Mix together the remaining olive oil, garlic, tomato puree, cherry tomatoes and mixed herbs. Add mixture to the vegetables and cook for a further 10 minutes or until fully cooked.
4   When cooked, turn the fryer off and leave vegetables inside for 5 minutes.
5   Season with salt & pepper and serve.

Roasted Root Vegetables 🌿
Serves 4

Ingredients

1 Carrot (cubed)
1 Parsnip (cubed)
1 Onion (cubed)
½ Celeriac Root (cubed)
½ Aubergine (cubed)
1 Cooked Beetroot (cubed)
1 Small Sweet Potato
2 Garlic Cloves (finely chopped))
2 tbsp Olive Oil
¼ Tsp dried Mixed Herbs

Method

1   Mix together the carrot, parsnip, onion, celeriac, beetroot, aubergine, sweet potato and 1 tbsp of olive oil in a bowl. Place into an ovenproof deep dish that is suitable for your air fryer.
2   Set the air fryer to 170°c (if applicable) and cook for 15 minutes. Remove from air fryer.
3   Mix together 1 tbsp of Oil, Garlic and mixed herbs, pour over vegetables and stir. Cook for a further 10 minutes or until fully cooked.
4   When cooked remove and season with salt & pepper.

Hedgehog Loaf
Serves 4

Ingredients

1 Bread Loaf or
4 Crusty rolls
or Tiger Loaf
(to fit size of
machine)
2 Garlic Cloves
(minced)
100g Butter
(softened)
1 tsp Mixed
Herbs
100g Brie
50g Chorizo (thinly sliced)
50g Grated Mozzarella

Method

1. Cut slits halfway through the loaf/rolls about 2 cm apart in a criss-cross pattern.
2. Mix the butter, garlic and mixed herbs. Fill each gap with the garlic butter mix and brush on top (to prevent burning).
3. Slice the brie into small chunks and stuff inside the gaps.
4. Push the sliced chorizo into any empty gaps.
5. Sprinkle the mozzarella over the top of the loaf.
6. Place in air fryer basket and cook at 170°c for 8-15 minutes until golden on top.

Why not change the brie & chorizo to bacon & cheddar or spinach, feta and sliced olives for a veggie option?

Dough Bites 🌿

Ingredients

225g Strong Plain Flour or Bread Flour
½ tsp Salt
1 tsp Caster Sugar
25g Melted Butter
150ml Lukewarm Milk
1 Packet of Dried Yeast

Method

1 Mix the yeast with the lukewarm milk and sugar and leave for 5 minutes.
2 Place the flour and salt into a bowl and mix in the melted butter.
3 Add the yeast liquid and knead for 5 minutes (or use mixer if you have one) to form a soft dough.
4 Place the dough into a bowl and cover with a clean, damp cloth and leave in a warm place for 15 minutes.
5 Knead the dough for a further 2 minutes to reduce it to its original size.
6 Roll the dough into balls (about golf ball size) and dust with flour.
7 Place on a suitable tray.
8 Cook at 170°c for 10 minutes turning after 3 minutes.

A **Cornbread:** Add 100g of creamed sweetcorn at stage 4 mixing it in and then follow the rest of the recipe.
B **Corn Dogs:** Make corn bread as above (A) and add a hot dog piece to the middle of each dough ball then follow the rest of the recipe.
C **Cheesy Chorizo Dough Bites:** Place a piece of your favourite cheese and some cubed chorizo into the centre of the dough ball at stage 6.
D **Garlic Dough Balls:** Brush with garlic butter for the last 2 minutes of cooking.
Instead of making the dough, you can use a ready-made bread mix.

Peshwari Naan 🌿

Ingredients

Basic Naan Dough
(*see below*) plus...
50g Desiccated
Coconut
25g Sultanas
2 tbsp Double Cream
10g Caster Sugar
(*Nigella/Black Onion Seeds. Seeds
as an optional topping*).

Method

1 Make basic naan dough, roll out thinly to double the size.
2 Mix the coconut, sultanas, sugar and cream together and spread onto one side of the rolled-out naan.
3 Fold the other side of the naan over so Peshwari mix is in the middle.
4 Follow steps 4 & 5 from basic Naan recipe.

Why not try alternative fillings, such as cheese, garlic & coriander, or mushroom?

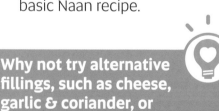

Basic Naan Bread 🌿
Ingredients

125g Self Raising Flour
2 tbsp Plain Yogurt
Salt
Cooking Spray
1 tsp Butter (melted)

Method

1 Pre-heat the air fryer basket at 170°c while making the naan.
2 Blend together the flour, yogurt, and a pinch of salt into a dough.
3 Roll out dough on a floured surface and shape into two ovals, that will fit into your air fryer basket.
4 Spray the basket with oil, place the naan bread in basket, spray with oil and cook at 170°c for 8-10 minutes, turning halfway through cooking.
5 Brush with melted butter.

Croissants 🌱
Serves 4

Ingredients
350g Pack
Croissant
Dough
Spray Oil

Fillings
1 slice Ham
30g Grated
Cheddar
Cheese.
30g Brie
1 tsp Cranberry Sauce.
30g Cheddar Cheese
6 Spinach Leaves.
50g Chocolate Chips (Dark & Milk).
50g Sultanas or Raisins
½ tsp Cinnamon.
1 tbsp of Jam (any Flavour).

Method

1   Unroll the dough and separate into triangles using a knife or pizza cutter.
2   Add the filling of your choice from above or leave plain.
3   Roll the croissant from the smaller side to the opposite corner to form a crescent.
4   Spray the air fryer basket with oil and lay the croissant in singe layers with space in between (may need to cook in batches) and spray the top of the croissants with spray oil.
5   Cook at 160°c for 6-8 minutes. Gently loosen from basket and cook for a further 1-3 minutes or until golden brown.

Toasted Tortilla Sandwich 🌿
Serves 1

Ingredients
1 Tortilla Wrap
Spray Oil

Choice of Fillings
2 slices Cooked Bacon
25g Cheddar (grated).
Sliced Stilton or sliced Brie.
2 slices of Ham.
50g Cooked Chicken (sliced).
½ Avocado (sliced).
25g Refined Beans.
50g Cooked Meat Balls (diced).
Sauces: BBQ Sauce, Mayonnaise, Mustard.
½ tsp Mixed Herbs

Method

1 Take your wrap and make a single cut from the centre to one edge.
2 Choose 4 fillings for your wrap and put one in each of the four quarters of the wrap. Cheese is best in the second/third quarter, (make sure you put any sauce on before adding cheese).
3 Fold the wrap from the first quarter of the wrap near the cut and then fold onto each quarter to form a triangle.
4 Spray the air fryer basket with oil and place the wrap into the basket.
5 Spray the top of the wrap with oil and cook at 180°c for 8-10 minutes, until golden brown.

Toasted Sandwich 🌿
Serves 1

Ingredients

2 slices of Bread
1 tbsp Butter or Margarine

Choice of Fillings

2 slices Cooked Bacon.
25g Cheddar (grated), sliced Stilton or sliced Brie.
2 slices of Ham.
50g Cooked Chicken (sliced).
½ Avocado (sliced).
50g Cooked Meat Balls (diced).
30g Sun Dried Tomatoes (diced).
Sauces: BBQ Sauce, Mayonnaise, Mustard.

Method

1. Butter your bread both sides and place on a board. Make sure you butter all the way to the edges on the outside top and bottom to stop the crusts from burning.
2. Choose the filling for your sandwich. Spread one side of the bread with sauce and place your filling of choice on top.
3. Place the other buttered piece of bread on top.
4. Place into the basket and cook at 180°c for 8-10 minutes, until golden brown.

My favourite filling is cream cheese spread on one slice, topped with grated Cheddar, sweet chilli sauce spread on the other slice, sandwich together and toast as above, Heaven, yum yum.

Easy Croque Monsieur
Serves 1

Ingredients

2 tablespoons Unsalted Butter, (softened)
2 slices White Bread
¼ tsp Dijon Mustard *(optional)*
2 thin slices Ham
50g Cheddar (grated)

Method

1   Butter one side of each slice of bread and place buttered side down on a clean cutting board.
2   Spread Dijon mustard on one of the slices. Arrange 2 slices of ham and 40g Cheddar on top of the Dijon.
3   Place the other slice of bread on top and top with the other 10g Cheddar or for added luxury, pour 3 tbsp of Bechamel Sauce on top and then top with cheese.
4   Place in air fryer basket and cook at 180°c for 5-8 minutes until cheese is melted and golden. Serve immediately.

Bechamel Recipe

Ingredients

25g Butter
25g Plain Flour
250ml Warm Milk
Pinch of Salt
Pinch of Ground Nutmeg

Method

1   Melt butter in a small saucepan over medium-low heat. Add flour and cook, stirring constantly, for 1-2 minutes until it makes a thick paste (roux).
2   Slowly pour in milk, whisking constantly and thoroughly, ensuring you get all of the roux from the bottom and edges of the pan.
3   Continue whisking and bring sauce to a simmer, then reduce heat to low and cook until sauce is thick enough to coat the back of a spoon, about 3 minutes.
4   Season sauce with salt and nutmeg. Reduce heat as low as possible and keep warm while preparing sandwiches.

Alternative fillings:
Smoked salmon & hollandaise · Beef tomato and mixed herbs · Stilton or blue cheese · Chicken breast & mayonnaise.

Egg Muffins
Makes 2-4

Ingredients
2 Large Eggs
50ml Milk
Salt & Pepper

Choice of Fillings
2 slices Cooked Bacon (diced).
25g Cheddar (grated) or crumbled Stilton.
2 slices of Ham (diced).
50g Cooked Chicken (diced).
½ Onion (diced).
½ Pepper (diced).
½ Avocado (sliced).
50g Cooked Sausages (diced).

Method

1   In a large bowl whisk the eggs with the milk and season with salt and pepper.
2   Mix in the fillings of your choice.
3   Pour the mixture into silicone cupcake cases, fill almost to the top.
4   Place into the basket and cook at 180°c for 8-10 minutes, until golden brown.

Make in advance. Cool and store in an airtight container in the fridge, they are great for a quick breakfast on the go or a healthy snack.

Roasted Soups

Serves 2

Ingredients

Roasted Vegetable of your choice
½ Onion (finely diced)
1 medium Potato (peeled & cubed)
1 tbsp Oil
¼ Garlic Granules
1 Vegetable/Chicken Stock Cube
(600ml boiling water)
Salt & Pepper

Method

1   In an ovenproof dish suitable for your air fryer, add the oil, vegetable options of your choice, onion and potato. Season with salt & pepper. Place in the air fryer and cook at 160°c for 10-15 minutes, until soft and slightly golden.
2   Meanwhile, make up your stock with your stock cube and 600ml of boiling water.
3   Once vegetables are cooked remove from air fryer and allow to cool slightly then place in a food processor/blender.
4   Add 200ml of the stock to the vegetables, along with garlic, and herbs or puree from soup option.
5   Blend until smooth, adding more stock until you reach your required consistancy.

Roasted Vegetable Options

Butternut Squash:
400g Butternut Squash
(peeled & cubed)

Parsnip:
Parsnips (peeled & cubed)

Vegetable:
2 Carrots (peeled & cubed)
& ¼ Swede (peeled & cubed)

Leek & Potato:
1 Leek (sliced)

Root Vegetable:
1 Carrot, 1 Sweet Potato, 1 Parsnip
(peeled & cubed)

Roasted Tomato:
400g Tomatoes (cubed and seeds removed), 1 tbsp Tomato Puree & ¼ tsp Mixed Herbs

Quick Chilli Cheese Nachos 🌿

Ingredients

100g Grated cheese
100ml Double Cream
1 tbsp Sweet Chilli Sauce
100g Tortilla Chips/Nachos

Method

1   Place all the sauce ingredients into a suitable oven proof dish.
2   Cook at 180°c for 6 minutes stirring every 2 minutes.
3   Put the tortilla chips in a suitable serving dish and pour the sauce over.

Sprinkle over some jalapeño peppers for an extra kick.
Why not use this cheese sauce over cauliflower, pasta, or over
a toasted sandwich to turn it into a variation of a croque monsieur?
Pour over chips, for cheesy chips.

Peanut Pork Balls

Serves 2-4

Ingredients

250g Minced Pork
1 Egg Yolk
1 Garlic Clove (minced)
1 tsp Cumin Powder
1 tbsp Sweet Chilli Sauce
75g Salted Peanuts
Cooking Spray

Method

1. In a bowl, mix together the minced pork, garlic, cumin powder, sweet chilli sauce and egg, stir to combine.
2. Roughly chop the salted peanuts in a food processor or place in a food back and bash with a rolling pin. Place the crushed nuts into a shallow bowl.
3. Roll the mince mixture into balls (around 8 balls) and coat with the chopped nuts.
4. Spray the air fryer basket with oil and place the pork balls into basket. Spray the tops with spray oil.
5. Cook at 180°c for 10-15 minutes, checking during cooking. Once the topping is golden remove from the air fryer.

Great served as a starter with sweet chilli dipping sauce or as an appetiser.

Tortilla Chicken Dippers
Serves 2

Ingredients

1 Chicken Breast
1 Egg
1 tsp Garlic Granules
1 tsp Soy Sauce
1 tsp Paprika
50g Tortilla Chips (crushed)
Cooking Spray
Salt & Pepper

Method

1   Cover the chicken with cling film and lightly bash, to flatten slightly.
2   Remove chicken from cling film, cut into strips and season with salt & pepper.
3   In a bowl, beat the egg with soy sauce and garlic granules. In another bowl place the crushed tortilla chips.
4   Coat the chicken in the egg mixture and then dip into the crushed tortilla chips and completely coat chicken.
5   Spray the air fryer basket with oil and place the chicken into basket. Spray the top of the chicken with extra oil.
6   Cook at 180°c for 10-15 minutes, checking during cooking. Once the chicken is cooked through and golden, remove from the air fryer.

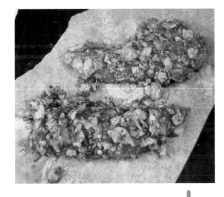

Use different flavour tortilla chips as an alternative. Great served with the BBQ sauce, garlic mayonnaise or your favourite dipping sauce.

Why not try Baby Bell individual cheeses instead of chicken fillets and decrease cooking time to 6 to 7 minutes.

Chinese Spare Ribs

Serves 2-4

Ingredients

500g Pork Ribs
50ml Hoisin Sauce
25ml Soy Sauce
2 tbsp Brown Sugar
1 tbsp Honey
1 tsp Five Spice Powder
½ tsp Garlic Powder
½ tsp Ginger Puree or grated Ginger.
1 tsp Paprika
Salt & Pepper

Method

1   Boil the ribs in water for 60-75 minutes until tender. Drain thoroughly and place in a large mixing bowl.
2   Mix together the hoisin sauce, soy sauce, brown sugar, honey, five spice, garlic, ginger, paprika and season with salt & pepper. Pour over ribs and stir to coat.
3   Place the ribs in the air fryer in a single layer ensuring they all cook evenly. (may need to cook in batches). Keep the remaining marinade to coat ribs halfway through.
4   Cook at 180°c for 15-20 minutes, turning the ribs halfway adding left over marinade.

Serve topped with chopped spring onions and rice.

Sweet Chilli Scallops and Prawns

Serves 2

Ingredients

8 Large Scallops
200g Raw Peeled King Prawns
50g Butter (cubed)
½ Lemon (juice)
½ Lemon (cut into 4 wedges)
2 tbsp Sweet Chilli Sauce
½ Garlic Clove (finely chopped)
1 tsp Mixed Herbs

Method

1. In a large bowl add the scallops, prawns, lemon juice, sweet chilli sauce, garlic and mixed herbs and mix together.
2. Place the mixture into an ovenproof deep dish suitable for your air fryer.
3. Add the cubes of butter over the mixture and add lemon wedges.
4. Cook at 180°c for 6-10 minutes, checking halfway.
5. Serve with fresh bread for dipping.

Great served over cooked spaghetti.

Add 2 tbsp of double cream to recipe at the end (remove lemon wedges) and stir, add mashed potatoes on top and return to air fryer for 5 minutes for a delicious seafood pie dish.

Great as an appetiser or starter

Alternative Filling:
50g Gruyere cheese, thinly sliced.
1 tsp English mustard
1 tsp honey
1 onion, thinly sliced and fried.

Stuffed Sirloin Steak Lollipops
Serves 2

Ingredients
200g Sirloin Steak
1 tbsp Harissa Paste *(optional)*
50g Mozzarella (grated)
50g Panko Breadcrumbs
4 rashers of Streaky Bacon
½ tsp Garlic Salt
Spray Oil
Cocktail Sticks
Baking Parchment
Tin Foil

Method

1   Wrap the steak in cling film and bash to 3mm thickness with a rolling pin.
2   Take the steak and spread on the harissa paste *(optional)*, and sprinkle on the mozzarella, panko breadcrumbs and garlic salt granules to cover the entire steak. Place the bacon rashers on top and roll into a swiss roll.

3   Take a piece of baking parchment and place on top of a piece of tin foil. Spray the parchment with oil.
4   Place the steak onto the parchment and roll the parchment and tin foil around the stuffed steak and pinch ends like a cracker.
5   Cook on 170°c for-   Rare 8 minutes
                          Medium 12 minutes,
                          Well done 15 minutes

This is a rough guide & will depend on the thickness of the meat. Once your steak is done to your liking, remove and let it rest keeping in the tin foil for 10 minutes.
6   Once rested, carefully unwrap and place steak onto a chopping board.
7   Cut the steak into 2 inch slices and insert a cocktail stick in each one.

Baked Camembert with Chorizo and Sweet Chilli Sauce

Serves 1-2

Ingredients

1 round Camembert
50g diced Chorizo
25g Butter (chopped)
3 tbsp Sweet Chilli Sauce
1 sprig of Rosemary
1 Garlic Clove

Method

1 Remove all packaging from the camembert and place the whole camembert in the centre of an ovenproof deep dish that is suitable for your air fryer.
2 Make a small hole in the centre of the camembert and put in the whole garlic clove and a sprig of rosemary.
3 Sprinkle the diced chorizo around the camembert, cover with sweet chilli sauce and place the chopped butter around the dish.
4 Cook in the air fryer at 180°c for 6-8 minutes or until cooked.
5 Remove from air fryer and plate. Serve with warm crusty bread or crudites.

Make this into an indulgent pasta by mixing all together into a sauce as soon as it is removed from air fryer. Serve over your favourite pasta.

Cauliflower Wings 🌿
Serves 2

Ingredients

1 small head of Cauliflower

75g Butter

1 tsp Hot Sauce *(optional)*

75g Panko Breadcrumbs or Crushed Tortilla Chips

1 tsp Garlic Powder

½ tsp dried Parsley

1 Spring Onion

50g Sour Cream

Method

1. Cut Cauliflower into bite sized pieces and place in a bowl.
2. Melt the butter and add in the hot sauce *(optional)*, garlic and parsley.
3. Pour over cauliflower and stir well.
4. Add the panko breadcrumbs or finely crushed tortilla chips and stir until coated.
5. Place the cauliflower bites into the air fryer basket in single layers (may need to cook in batches).
6. Cook at 170°c For 10-15 minutes, stopping halfway through to turn cauliflower. If you would like them crispier, cook for a further 2-3 minutes.
7. Sprinkle over some chopped spring onions and serve with a side salad. Add sour cream for dipping.

For extra heat, add additional hot sauce.

Scotch Eggs
Serves 4

Ingredients
5 Eggs
300g Pork Sausage Meat
100g Breadcrumbs
110g Plain Flour
Spray Oil

Method

1   Boil 4 of the eggs for 10 minutes. Cool them in ice cold water and remove the shells.
2   Place the flour in one bowl, a beaten egg in another bowl and the breadcrumbs in another bowl.
3   Divide the sausage meat into four balls.
4   Mould the sausage meat around each hardboiled egg.
5   Then roll each one into the flour, then the egg and then the breadcrumbs.
6   Place them into the air fryer basket and spray with oil.
7   Cook at 180°c for 15-20 minutes, turning halfway through.

For soft boiled eggs, boil for 6 mins in step one.

Onion Bhaji
Serves 4

Ingredients

75g Gram Flour (chickpea flour)
175g Onions (finely sliced)
100g Carrots (finely grated)
½ Paprika
1 tbsp Coriander
1 tsp Cumin
½ tsp Curry Powder
1 Lemon (juice)
Spray Oil
Salt & Pepper

Method

1   In a large mixing bowl, mix together the gram flour, onions, carrots, paprika, coriander, cumin, curry powder, lemon juice and a pinch of salt & pepper, to form a dough. *(Add water if required)*.
2   Shape the mixture into bite sized balls.
3   Place the balls in the air fryer and spray with oil.
4   Cook at 180°c for 10-15 minutes, checking and respraying with oil every 5 mins until golden brown.

**Add some sliced chillies to the mixture for extra heat.
Great as a starter or as a side dish to a curry.**

Sesame Seed Sausage Rolls
Makes 12

Ingredients
320g Ready Rolled Puff pastry
1 Onion (finely chopped)
225g Pork Sausage Meat
1 tbsp Cranberry Sauce
½ tsp Mixed Herbs
1 tbsp Sesame seeds
1 Egg to glaze

Method

1   Mix together the sausage meat, herbs, onion, cranberry, salt & pepper in a bowl.
2   Roll out puff pastry and cut into 12 rectangles.
3   Place each on a baking parchment, then roll some sausage meat mixture and place on the rectangle of pastry. Glaze edge with beaten egg and fold pastry over the top.
4   Score the top of the pastry and glaze the top with egg and sprinkle with sesame seeds.
5   Place in batches into the air fryer basket, cooking at 170°c for 8-10 minutes or until golden brown and thoroughly cooked.

Why not substitute the cranberry sauce for sweet pickle and a finely chopped apple?

Make it vegetarian by replacing the sausage meat with 100g grated cheese and 125g grated carrot.

Filo Money Bags
Makes 10

Ingredients
270g Filo pastry (cut into 30 squares)
200g Pork Mince
1 tbsp Oil
4 Red Onions (finely chopped)
1 tbsp Sweet Pickle
(Branston's/Ploughman's)
13g Melted Butter for brushing

Method

1 Fry off the pork mince in a pan with 1 tbsp of oil for 5-8 minutes until golden brown. Add the red onion, sweet pickle, season with salt & pepper and remove from the heat.
2 Lay the filo pastry out and cut into squares. Take one of the squares and place another on top at a 45 degree angle then repeat once more, so you have 3 filo squares on top of each other.
3 Place a spoonful of the mince mix in the centre, moisten the edge with a little water and pull up the corners to make a parcel.
4 Repeat until all 10 are complete.
5 Brush parcels with melted butter.
6 Place a single layer of the parcels into the air fryer (this may need to be done in two batches).
7 Cook at 170°c for 5-10 minutes until golden brown.

For a Vegetarian option, replace the pork mince with 200g crumbled feta cheese.

Chinese Dumplings

Serves 4-6

Filling

175g Pork Mince
75g Prawns (finely chopped)
1 Garlic Clove (peeled and chopped)
2 tsp Sweet Chilli Sauce
1 cm Fresh Ginger (peeled and chopped)
½ tbsp Sesame Seed Oil
½ tbsp Soy Sauce
½ tsp Sugar
1 Egg Yolk
1 tsp Rice Vinegar
1 Onion (peeled & finely chopped)
2 tbsp Cornflour
Spray Oil

Ingredients

200g Plain Flour
50g Cornflour
125ml Water
½ tsp Salt

Method

1   In a bowl mix the minced pork, prawns, chopped ginger, garlic, onion, sesame seed oil, soy sauce, sweet chilli sauce, sugar, egg yolk, rice vinegar, cornflour. Season and set aside.
2   To make dough place the flour, cornflour, salt and 80ml of water into food processor and blend (this can be done by hand).
3   Add 30ml of water and blend to a breadcrumb consistency.
4   Add the last 15ml of water then mould together into a dough.
5   Roll into 15 separate balls. Roll each ball flat ready for the meat mixture.
6   Place a tsp of the meat mixture into each flattened dough piece.
7   Wet edges with water, fold up and seal them together into dumplings.
8   Spray well with oil so they are completely coated and place in a suitable tin for an air fryer.
9   Place the dumplings into the air fryer baskets and cook at 170°c for 10 minutes, checking every 5 mins and respraying with oil (this may need to be done in batches).
10 Turn all the dumplings over and respray with oil. Cook for a further 5-10 minutes until golden brown.

Mains

Sausage Provençal
Serves 4

Ingredients

6 Pork Sausages
1 Onion (sliced)
50ml Red Wine
400g Tinned Chopped Tomatoes
1 Red Pepper (diced)
1 tsp Mixed Herbs
1 tsp Paprika
2 Garlic Cloves (chopped)
4tbsp Tomato Ketchup or Tomato Puree
1 Chicken Stock cube
100ml Boiling Water

Method

1 Mix the sausages, onion, red pepper, mixed herbs, paprika and garlic puree together and place into an ovenproof deep dish that is suitable for your air fryer.
2 Cook at 170°c for 10 minutes until sausages are browned.
3 Add the red wine, stir and cook for a further 5 minutes.
4 Add the tomato ketchup/puree, chopped tomatoes and chicken stock (stock cube mixed with 100ml of boiling water).
5 Cook for a further 20 minutes stirring every 5-10 minutes.
6 Season with salt & pepper and serve with mashed potato, boiled rice, jacket potato or potato wedges and vegetables.

As an alternative, why not change the sausages for 4 chicken thighs (skinned, boned and diced) or vegan sausages with a vegetable stock cube?

For gluten free, choose gluten free sausages, gluten free stock cubes and use tomato puree.

Bacon & Chorizo Burgers
Serves 4

Ingredients

500g Minced Beef

50g Chorizo (diced)

1 Onion (finely chopped)

1 tbsp Sweet Pickle (Branston's/Ploughman's)

1 tsp Garlic Granules

1 Egg

1 tbsp Plain Flour

12 slices of Streaky Bacon

Topping choices:

Cheddar Cheese, Stilton or Brie.

Onion Rings.

Lettuce & Tomato.

Mayonnaise.

Method

1 Chop the sweet pickle to a fine consistency (*like you would chop parsley on a chopping board*).
2 Mix all the ingredients together in a bowl. Save the bacon for wrapping.
3 Form into four burgers.
4 Lay 4 slices of bacon on your board in a lattice pattern and place a burger on top and wrap the excess bacon over the top of the burger. Repeat for the other 3.

5 Cook at 170°c for 20-25 minutes turning halfway through cooking. Serve in a seed burger bun with toppings of your choice and chips.

For a bacon and mushroom burger, swap the Chorizo with mushrooms. For a low fat option, swap the minced beef with minced turkey and the chorizo with cranberry sauce.

You can use pork, lamb or turkey mince for your meatballs.
Leave out the chilli for a non-spicy version.

Use cornflour in the meatballs and crushed
tortilla chips for the topping to create a gluten free dish.

Meat Balls in a Spicy Tomato Sauce
Serves 4

Ingredients
500g Minced Beef
1 Onion (finely chopped)
3 tbsp of Plain Flour
1 Egg
1 tsp Garlic Granules
Salt & Black Pepper
1 tbsp Oil
1 tbsp Chilli Powder
4 tbsp Tomato Ketchup
2 tbsp Tomato Puree
1 Garlic Clove (finely chopped)
4 tsp Mixed Herbs
2 tins Chopped Tomatoes
4 Tomatoes (quartered)

Topping
65g Breadcrumbs
65g Parmesan

Method
1 Place the mince, black pepper, egg, garlic, salt and ½ onion in a large bowl. Mix these together and slowly begin to add the flour, mixing all the time.
2 Once all the flour has been added, roll the mixture into balls (just smaller than a ping pong ball). Use a little extra flour to dust hands if necessary.
3 Place the meatballs, remaining onion and oil into a deep ovenproof dish suitable for an air fryer.
4 Cook at 170°c for 15-20 minutes, until onions are soft and meat balls are browned.
5 Mix together the chilli powder, garlic, garlic granules, tomato ketchup, tomato purée, mixed herbs, chopped tomatoes and quartered tomatoes.
6 Add to meat balls and cook for a further 20-25 minutes.
7 Mix together the breadcrumbs and parmesan cheese, sprinkle on top of the meat balls and cook for a further 10-15 minutes until golden brown.

Steak with Creamy Stilton Sauce

Serves 1

Ingredients

1 thin cut Sirloin Steak (110g)
½ Onion (sliced)
1 tsp Olive Oil
¼ tsp Garlic Salt
1 tsp Ground Black Pepper
100g Stilton Cheese
1 tsp of Sweet Pickle (Branston's/Ploughman's)
100ml of Double Cream
1 tbsp fresh Parsley

Method

1   Mix the garlic salt & ground black pepper together, rub onto both sides of steak. Place into an ovenproof deep dish suitable for your air fryer.
2   Mix the onions with the olive oil & spread around the steak.
3   Cook on 170°c for —   Rare 3 minutes on each side,
                           Medium 6 minutes on each side,
                           Well done 9 minutes on each side
    This is a rough guide & will depend on the thickness of the meat.
    Once your Steak is done to your liking, remove and let rest. Keep onions for serving (cover with tin foil to keep hot).
4   Crumble the stilton, add the pickle and cream and return to the air fryer in the ovenproof dish for approx. 5 minutes, stirring every minute of the cooking time.
5   Top the Steak with the cooked onions and creamy stilton sauce and sprinkle with chopped fresh parsley. Serve with chips, mushrooms and salad.

Swap steak for a turkey steak or pork loin steak.
Cook both for approx. 8 minutes on each side at 170°c.
For a gluten free option, replace the pickle.

Roast Beef with Suet Crust
Serves 2-4

Ingredients

600g Beef Joint
½ Onion (finely diced)
75g Beef Suet
150g Self Raising Flour
1 tsp Mixed Herbs
1 tbsp Beef Gravy Granules
1 tbsp Oil
Salt & Pepper

Method

1. Season the beef joint with salt & pepper and rub with oil.
2. Place the beef joint in an ovenproof deep dish that is suitable for your air fryer. Cook at 170°c for 25-35 minutes, turning every 10 minutes.
3. Mix the flour, suet, diced onion and mixed herbs with a little cold water to form a dough. Mould the suet into a thick sausage shape. Remove the basket from the air fryer and place the suet dough next to the joint of beef.
4. Place basket back in air fryer and cook at 170°c for another 10 minutes, checking every 5 minutes.
5. Remove the beef joint and leave to rest. Cook the suet crust for a further 10 minutes until lightly golden. Remove the suet to serve.
6. Add the gravy granules to the juice in the bottom of the dish and stir, add enough boiling water until your preferred consistency is achieved.
7. Carve beef joint and serve with suet crust, potatoes and vegetables topped with the delicious gravy.

Reduce or increase the recipe to the size of your air fryer.

Reduce the cooking time of the joint in step 4 to 20 minutes for a rare beef or increase to 45 minutes for well done.

Rack of Lamb with Herb Crust
Serves 2

Ingredients

1 Rack of Lamb
2 tbsp Honey
½ tsp English Mustard
2 tsp dried Parsley
2 tsp dried Thyme
2 tsp dried Rosemary
1 Slice of Granary Bread
Spray Oil

Method

1. Finely chop the bread into crumbs or blend in a food processor.
2. Mix the breadcrumbs with parsley, thyme and rosemary.
3. Mix the honey and mustard together, coat the rack of lamb and roll it into the crumb mixture.
4. Spray your air fryer basket with spray oil.
5. Place the lamb into the basket, spray the crust with oil and cook at 170°c for 25-30 minutes, until golden and crisp.

This herb crust would go great on lamb steak or pork Chops.

For alternative lamb chops see our Moroccan marinade on page 8. Serve with cous cous and cucumber & mint Salad.

Lamb Chops in Mint Jelly
Serves 2

Ingredients

6 Lamb Chops
2 tbsp Mint Jelly
1 tbsp Oil
Salt & Pepper

Method

1. Mix together the oil, mint jelly, a pinch of salt & pepper and 1 tbsp of boiling water in a bowl.
2. Place the lamb chops in the mint mixture making sure they are well covered. Leave the chops to marinate for 30 mins in the fridge.
3. Place the chops in an oven proof dish suitable for your air fryer and spoon over any remaining mint mixture.
4. Cook at 180°c for 10 minutes for rare and 15 minutes for well done.
5. Serve with creamy mashed potatoes and seasonal vegetables.

Pork Stuffed with Gammon
Serves 4

Ingredients

1.2kg Pork Joint
330g Gammon Steak (cut in two)
200g Tinned Pineapple Pieces in Juice (chopped)
85g Sage and Onion Stuffing Mix
Pinch Salt & Pepper
Fresh Parsley
100mls Boiling Water

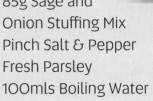

Method

1   Add 100mls of boiling water to stuffing mix and stir. Add the pineapple and mix.
2   Cut open the pork joint so that it is almost into two pieces but still held together by the fat.
3   Place the gammon pieces in this gap (each side) and fill with the stuffing.
4   Roll up and tie with butcher's string, spray with oil and rub skin with salt.
5   Place in a tin suitable for an air fryer at 170°c for
    1 - 1 ½ hours, or until cooked, turning every 20 minutes.

For extra indulgence, add the meat from two skinned sausages in step 1. Change the pineapple to one cored, peeled and chopped apple.

Chicken & Lamb with Sage & Onion Stuffing

Serves 3-4

Ingredients

2 Chicken Breasts
240g Lamb Neck Fillet
1 Pork Sausage (skinned)
4 Slices Prosciutto Ham
2 tbsp Sage & Onion Stuffing Mix
13g Butter
2 Cloves Garlic (chopped)
2 tbsp Honey
1 tsp Mustard
1 tbsp Chopped Fresh Parsley
100ml of Boiling Water
Kitchen String & Kitchen Foil

Method

1. Mix together the butter, garlic, parsley, honey and mustard in a bowl.
2. In a separate bowl put the sage and onion stuffing mix with 100ml of boiling water and mix together. Add the sausage meat and combine.
3. On a large sheet of foil pour the honey and garlic mixture in the centre and lay the prosciutto ham out in lines over the top.
4. Place the lamb in middle with the two chicken breasts either side and place the stuffing/sausage mix on top of the lamb.
5. Roll up and tie with the string then wrap with the foil.
6. Place in the air fryer basket and cook at 170°c for 45 minutes. Allow to rest for 20 minutes (in the foil) and serve.

Baked Potato and Eggs
Serves 2

Ingredients

2 Large Baking Potatoes
100g Smoked Bacon Lardons
½ Onion (finely chopped)
2 Cloves Garlic (finely chopped)
50g Baby Spinach
2 Large Eggs
20ml Milk
100g Cheddar Cheese (grated)
100ml Plain Greek Yogurt
2 tbsp Spring Onion (chopped)

Method

1   Wash the baking potatoes, spray with cooking oil and season with salt & pepper (do not pierce the potatoes). Place in air fryer basket and cook at 175°c for 40 minutes, checking them halfway through and turn them over.
2   Meanwhile, spray a frying pan with spray oil and fry bacon lardons for 5-10 minutes until crispy. Transfer to a paper towel.
3   In the same pan fry the onions and garlic on a medium heat for 2 minutes, add spinach and sauté for 3 minutes, until wilted. Remove from heat.
4   Once the potatoes are cooked, allow to cool.
5   Cut an oval in the top of each potato and scoop out the potato with a spoon, being careful not to pierce the skin of the potato.
6   Mould the base of your potato skin being careful not to break the skin to ensure they have a good base to stand evenly.
7   Divide the bacon and spinach mix between the two potatoes.
8   Whisk the eggs with the milk and add 80g of Cheddar and pour ½ into each potato and top with remaining Cheddar.
9   Place in the air fryer basket and cook at 175°c for 15-20 minutes, until cheese is golden brown.
10 In a bowl combine the spring onions and greek yogurt, serve with the potatoes.

Stuffed Peppers
Serves 2

Ingredients

2 Peppers (red or green)
200g Minced Beef
½ Onion (finely chopped)
2 Mushrooms (finely chopped)
125g Long Grain Rice (cooked)
4 tsp Paprika
4 tsp Garlic Salt
1 tbsp Tomato Puree
25g Parmesan Cheese (grated)
25g Breadcrumbs

Method

1   Fry the minced beef in a pan for 5-8 minutes until browned. Add in onion, paprika, garlic salt and tomato puree, stir and cook for another 5 minutes.
2   In a separate bowl, mix the mushrooms, parmesan cheese, breadcrumbs and cooked rice (save a little parmesan and breadcrumbs for sprinkling later). Pour into the mince mixture, season well with salt and pepper and stir.
3   Slice off the tops of the 2 peppers and set aside. Scoop out any seeds. Trim the base of the pepper so they stand up.
4   Fully fill each pepper to the brim with the stuffing mixture and press down well.
5   Mix the remaining parmesan & breadcrumbs together and sprinkle on top of each pepper.
6   Put the lids back on the peppers and place in the air fryer basket.
7   Cook at 170°c for 15 minutes, checking every 5 minutes.
8   Serve with a mixed salad.

Chestnut mushrooms work best with this recipe.

For a heathier option replace the minced beef for turkey mince.

Make it vegan! Use veggie mince and replace the parmesan with vegan hard cheese.

Stuffed Courgettes
Serves 2

Ingredients

2 medium
Courgettes
1 tbsp Oil
1 Onion (finely
chopped)
1 Green Pepper
(diced)
250g Minced
Beef
1 tsp Mixed Herbs
1 tsp Paprika
1 Garlic Clove (minced)
300g Chopped Tomatoes
100g Breadcrumbs
100g Grated Mozzarella

Method

1. Cut the courgettes in half longways and scoop out the centres.
2. In a pan, over a medium heat fry the onion and green pepper until soft. Add in the minced beef and cook until browned.
3. Add the herbs, paprika, garlic and chopped tomatoes and stir to combine.
4. Share the meat mixture between the courgette halves and place them in the air fryer.
5. Cook at 170°c For 8-10 minutes. Mix mozzarella and breadcrumbs together and sprinkle on top of courgettes. Cook for a further 5-8 minute until cheese is melted and golden brown (this may need to be cooked in two batches, depending on the size of your air fryer).

Replace the minced beef for turkey mince, pork mince or veggie mince.

59

Southern Fried Chicken

Serves 4-6

Ingredients

8 Boneless and Skinless Chicken Thighs

Marinade

150ml (a pint) Sour Cream
½ tsp Celery Salt
1 tsp Cayenne Pepper
1 tsp White Pepper
1 tsp Cinnamon

Coating

6 tbsp Plain Flour
6 tbsp Breadcrumbs
1 tsp White Pepper
4 tsp Cinnamon
1 tsp Paprika
1 tsp Celery Salt

Method

1 Mix all marinade ingredients in a bowl and add the chicken pieces.
2 In another bowl place all the coating ingredients and mix.
3 Dip the marinated chicken in the coating ingredients until completely covered and place each piece carefully on a non-stick tray suitable for an air fryer.
4 Cook the chicken at 170°c for 15-20 minutes until golden and cooked through.

Make it spicy with 2 tsp of chilli powder (to your taste). Alternatively change chicken to pork steaks.
Spray cooked chicken with oil for extra indulgence.

Baked Chicken Caprese
Serves 2

Ingredients
2 Chicken Breasts or Boneless Thighs
1 tbsp Olive Oil
½ tsp dried Basil
½ tsp dried Oregano
¼ Garlic Powder
250g Cherry Tomatoes (cut in half)
1 Red Onion (diced)
2 tbsp Balsamic Vinegar
1 tbsp Brown Sugar
100g grated Mozzarella
Salt & Pepper

Method

1 Place chicken breasts/thighs in an ovenproof deep dish that is suitable for your air fryer. Sprinkle with olive oil, basil, oregano, garlic powder and season with salt & pepper.
2 Place the tomatoes and onions around the chicken breasts/thighs.
3 Mix the balsamic vinegar and brown sugar together and pour over the chicken.
4 Cook in air fryer at 170°c for 10-15 minutes depending on the thickness of the chicken breasts/thighs.
5 Add the mozzarella cheese on top of chicken breasts/thighs and cook for a further 5-10 minutes until the cheese is melted and golden brown.
6 Once cooked remove the chicken. Stir the remaining tomato mixture and serve over the chicken breasts/thighs.

Great with homemade potato wedges see page 18.

Whole Baked Chorizo Chicken

Ingredients

1 Whole Chicken
1 Garlic Clove (chopped)
50g Butter
¼ tsp Mixed Herbs
75g Chorizo Sausage (sliced and halved)
1 Lemon (cut in quarters)
Salt & Pepper

Method

1   To make the garlic butter, warm the butter to room temperature and mix in the herbs and chopped garlic.
2   Slice the chorizo sausage and cut slices in half.
3   Cut deep horizontal cuts in the chicken through the skin along the length of the breasts and legs.
4   Stuff these cuts with garlic butter and the chorizo - place the lemon quarters inside the chicken and season the chicken with salt & pepper.
5   Place the chicken in the air fryer on a suitable baking tray. Or if your fryer has a rotisserie spit use this instead. Cook at 170°c for 60-90 minutes or until cooked through. *If your fryer isn't big enough for a whole chicken use skin on breasts or thighs instead.*

Top Tips and Alternatives

A.   **BBQ chicken.** To give your chicken extra flavour, coat with BBQ marinade (see page 5), for the last 10 mins of cooking.
B.   **Tandoori chicken.** Add tandoori seasoning to your garlic butter and remove the chorizo for a whole tandoori chicken.
C.   **Coronation chicken.** Add a tsp of curry powder and a tsp of mango chutney to your garlic butter and use dried apricots instead of chorizo to make a delicious coronation style chicken.
D.   **Chorizo paprika chicken.** Follow the baked chorizo chicken recipe: Mix ½ tsp smoked paprika, ½ tsp olive oil and ½ tsp sweet chilli sauce and brush over your chicken 10 minutes before the end of cooking.

Katsu Chicken Curry
Serves 1

Ingredients
1 Chicken
Breast
1 Egg
50g Panko
Breadcrumbs
Cooking Spray
Salt & Pepper

Method

1. Cover the chicken with cling film and lightly bash, to flatten slightly.
2. Remove chicken from cling film and season with salt & pepper.
3. In a bowl, beat the egg. In another bowl, place the breadcrumbs.
4. Coat the chicken in the egg and then into the breadcrumbs.
5. Spray the air fryer basket with oil and place the breadcrumbed chicken into basket. Spray the top of the chicken with spray oil.
6. Cook at 180°c for 15-20 minutes, checking during cooking. Once the chicken is cooked through and the breadcrumbs are golden, remove from the air fryer. Serve with katsu curry sauce and rice of your choice.

Katsu Curry Sauce
Ingredients
1 tbsp Curry Powder
1 tsp Garam Masala
2 tsp Sweet Chilli Sauce
1 Diced Onion
1 tbsp Soy Sauce
1 Chicken Stock- made with a Stock Cube and 100ml Hot Water
50ml Double Cream

Method

1. In an ovenproof dish that fits into your air fryer, add in all the ingredients to dish, stir and cook at 170°c for 10-15 minutes, stirring every 5 minutes.

Cook your katsu curry sauce in advance for ease.

Tandoori Chicken
Serves 2

Ingredients

2 Chicken
Pieces
(drumstick and
thigh)
2 tbsp Tandoori
Spice Mix
250ml Plain
Yogurt
1 Lemon
(juiced)
1 tsp Garlic Granules
Spray Oil

Method

1   Mix together in a large bowl the yogurt, tandoori spices, lemon juice and garlic granules.
2   Place the chicken pieces in the yogurt mixture and coat well.
3   Cover with cling film and place in the fridge to marinate for 6 hours or overnight.
4   Spray an ovenproof dish suitable for your air fryer with cooking oil and place the chicken in.
5   Cook at 170°c for 45 minutes, until golden brown and cooked through.

Great served with naan bread from page 24 and rice of your choice.

Hawaiian Chicken
Serves 2

Ingredients

2 Chicken Breasts
4 Pineapple Rings
50g Mozzarella (grated)
6 slices of Bacon
Salt & Pepper

Method

1. Cover the chicken with cling film and bash to 1 inch thickness.
2. Remove chicken from cling film and season with salt & pepper.
3. Cut the pineapple rings in half and place on one half of the chicken breasts. Sprinkle over the mozzarella.
4. Fold the other half of the chicken over the pineapple
5. On a board, lay out 3 pieces of bacon per chicken breast, overlapping slightly.
6. Place the chicken on top of the bacon and wrap around.
7. Spray your air fryer basket with spray oil.
8. Place the breasts into the basket with the bacon fold at the bottom and cook at 170°c for 25-30 minutes, until golden and crisp.

Replace pineapple for tomato and basil for an Italian twist.

Replace the mozzarella and pineapple for garlic cream cheese for a Kiev style chicken dish.

Roast Duck with Hoisin Sauce
Serves 2

Ingredients

2 Duck Breasts

Marinade

1 tsp Chinese Five Spice
1tsp Sesame Seed Oil
1tsp Soy Sauce

For Hoisin Sauce

1 Garlic Clove (chopped)
1cm Fresh Ginger (chopped)
3 tbsp Hoisin Sauce
1 table Golden Syrup
1 tbsp Soy Sauce
1/2 tsp Chinese Five Spice
1 tbsp Rice Wine Vinegar
1 tsp Nigella Seeds *(optional)*

Method

1. Place all the sauce ingredients in a pan, stir and bring to the boil for five minutes and set aside.
2. Prick the duck breast skin lots of times with a fork and score lines across with a sharp knife to help release the fat when cooking.
3. Mix the marinade ingredients together and pour over the duck breast (this can be done in advance for a stronger flavour).
4. Place the duck breast on a suitable tray and cook at 200°c for 5 minutes skin side up, turn and cook for a further 3 minutes on other side.
5. Reduce the heat to 170°c turn the duck back to skin side up and brush the skin with 1 tsp of the sauce cook for 3 minutes for rare, 5 minutes for medium and 7 minutes for well-done. Rest for 5 minutes after cooking.
6. Slice the duck and pour over the sauce. Serve with egg noodles and vegetables of your choice.

For an alternative marinade, use our Chinese marinade recipe on page 5.

Chicken & Leek Puff Pastry Topped Pie

Serves 2

Ingredients

2 Chicken Breasts (diced)
2 Leeks (sliced)
1 Onion (diced)
1 Garlic Clove (finely chopped)
1 tbsp Olive Oil
100ml Chicken Stock (made with 1 stock cube and 100ml water)
1 tsp Plain Flour
100ml Double Cream
Salt & Pepper
160g Ready Rolled Puff Pastry
Beaten Egg or Milk for brushing Pastry.

Method

1. In an oven proof dish that fits into your air fryer, place the olive oil, onion, garlic, leeks and chicken. Season with salt & pepper. Cook at 170°c for 10 minutes, stirring every 5 minutes. Remove from air fryer.
2. Add the flour and stir, then add in the chicken stock and cook for a further 5 minutes. Remove from air fryer.
3. Add cream and stir well. Cook for another 5 minutes.
4. Roll out the pastry and cut a piece to fit on top of your dish.
5. Add the puff pastry on top of the chicken mixture and brush with milk or beaten egg.
6. Cook for a further 10 minutes until golden brown. Serve with potatoes and vegetables of your choice.

Add cubed ham and/or mushrooms for extra flavour in step one.

Turkey can be used instead of chicken.

Duck and Mushroom en Croute

Serves 2

Ingredients

320g Ready Rolled Puff Pastry
2 Duck Breasts
200g Mushrooms
1 Onion (finely diced)
1 tsp Golden Syrup
1 tbsp Hoisin Sauce
1 tsp Soy Sauce
Beaten Egg or Milk to glaze

Method

1 Roll out the pastry and cut into 4 equal rectangles.
2 Place 2 of the puff pastry rectangles on parchment paper and cook in air fryer at 170°c for 5-10 minutes.
3 Remove the skin from the duck and slice. Place the mushrooms, onions, sliced duck breast and skin in a dish suitable for air fryer and cook in air fryer at 170°c for 5-10 minutes, until onion is soft and duck is part cooked. Allow to cool.
4 On the part cooked pastry rectangles, place the onions, mushrooms, and then the duck.
5 Mix the golden syrup, hoisin and soy sauce together and pour over the duck.
6 Place the other pastry rectangles on top and crimp edges of pastry together using a fork. Cut leaves out of spare pastry for decoration (optional). Brush the top of the pastry with milk or beaten egg.
7 Cook in the air fryer basket at 170°c for 15-20 minutes, until golden brown. (may need to cook in batches or smaller size en croutes depending on the size of the air fryer).

Chicken en Croute Serves 2

320g Ready Rolled Puff Pastry
2 Chicken Breast
100g Bacon Lardons
1 Onion (sliced)
Milk/beaten egg (for wash)

Method

1 Roll out the pastry and cut into 4 equal rectangles.
2 Place 2 of the puff pastry rectangles on parchment paper and cook in air fryer at 170°c for 5-10 minutes.
3 Slice chicken and place in a dish suitable for air fryer with onions and bacon lardons and cook in air fryer at 170°c for 5-10 minutes, until onion is soft and chicken is part cooked. Allow to cool.
4 On the part cooked pastry rectangles, place the chicken mixture. Place the other pastry rectangle on top and crimp edges of pastry together with a fork. Brush the top of the pastry with milk or beaten egg.
5 Cook in the air fryer basket at 170°c for 15-20 minutes, until golden brown. (May need to cook in batches depending on the size of the air fryer).

Steak en Croute Serves 2

160g Ready Rolled Puff Pastry
300g Fillet Steak
75g Stilton Cheese
1 Red Onion, Sliced
Butter
Milk/beaten egg (for wash)

Method

1 Roll out the pastry and cut into 2 equal rectangles.
2 Place one of the puff pastry rectangles on parchment paper and cook in air fryer at 170°c for 5-10 minutes.
3 In a hot pan, place butter and sear steak for 2 minutes on each side. Allow to cool.
4 On the part cooked pastry rectangles, place the sliced onion and fillet steak and top with Stilton cheese. Place the other pastry rectangle on top and crimp edges of pastry together with a fork. Brush the top of the pastry with milk or beaten egg.
5 Cook in the air fryer basket at 170°c for 10-15 minutes, until golden brown. (May need to cook in batches depending on the size of the air fryer).

As an alternative try mediterranean vegetables, such as aubergine, yellow and green peppers, garlic, tomato, red onion with mixed herbs, mixed with olive oil and tomato puree as a filling.

69

Creamy Tomato, Chorizo & Prawn Spaghetti

Serves 2

Ingredients

200g Spaghetti
500ml Water
250g Cooked King Prawns
50g Chorizo (diced)
2 tbsp Garlic (chopped)
½ Onion (diced)
100g Cherry Tomatoes (halved)
1 Red Pepper (deseeded and diced)
1 tbsp Capers
1 tbsp Tomato Puree
1 tsp Mixed Herbs
50g grated Mozzarella
2 tbsp Mascarpone Cheese
2 tbsp Olive Oil

Method

1   Boil the water, once boiling, add spaghetti and cook as per the pack instructions (save a little water).
2   Meanwhile, in an ovenproof dish suitable for your air fryer, add the olive oil, peppers, onion, chorizo, cherry tomatoes and garlic. Place in the air fryer and cook at 170°c for 5-8 minutes until soft and slightly golden.
3   Add prawns, tomato puree, 50ml of pasta water, capers, and mixed herbs and cook at 170°c for a further 5-8 minutes until sauce is heated through.
4   Remove from the air fryer and stir in the mascarpone and mozzarella and cook for a further 2-5 minutes at 170°c until mozzarella has melted.
5   Add the sauce to the spaghetti and serve.

Add a handful of chilli flakes to step 3 to add some heat.

Roasted Garlic Tomato and Feta Pasta 🌿

Serves 2

Ingredients

70g Full Fat Feta Cheese Block
140g Cherry Tomatoes
½ Onion (chopped)
2 Garlic Cloves (finely chopped)
1 tsp Mixed Herbs
1 tbsp Olive Oil
150g Pasta of your Choice

Method

1   In an ovenproof deep dish that is suitable for your air fryer, toss together the cherry tomatoes, chopped onion, garlic, mixed herbs and most of the olive oil.

2   Add the feta cheese block into the middle of the tomatoes and splash with olive oil. Season with salt & pepper.

3   Place in the air fryer and cook at 170°c for 15-20 minutes, checking every 5 minutes, until the tomatoes are soft and golden brown and the feta is soft.

4   Cook the pasta as per pack instructions to al dente, reserve 50ml of pasta water.

5   Once the feta & tomatoes are ready, remove from air fryer and mash the feta and tomatoes into a smooth mixture.

6   Stir the mixture into the drained pasta and stir until fully coated. Add a little pasta water to the sauce if seems too dry.

If desired, add a handful of spinach when combining sauce with pasta.

Chicken with Cauliflower Pizza Base

Serves 1-2 | Carb & Gluten Free

Ingredients

1 Chicken Breast
½ Head of Cauliflower
50g Parmesan Cheese
1 Egg
1 tsp Garlic Salt
Pizza sauce
(see page 10)
Mozzarella
Pizza Toppings of your Choice

Method

1   Place the chicken in a food processor and blend to a paste. Add in the cauliflower, parmesan and egg. Blend until mixture forms a paste.
2   On a piece of parchment, spread out half of the mixture and shape into a circle of ½ cm thickness to a slightly smaller size than your air fryer basket. Repeat for second base.
3   Cook at 180°c for 8-10 minutes, checking during cooking until lightly browned.
4   Add pizza sauce and mozzarella, with toppings of your choice.
5   Return to the air fryer and cook at 180°c for a further 10 minutes.
6   Once the topping and crust is golden, remove from the air fryer and serve.

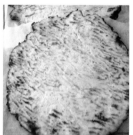

For a vegetarian version, remove the chicken and use the whole head of the cauliflower.

Cheats Pizza Base
Serves 2

Ingredients

225g Self Raising Flour
50g Olive Oil
50g Cheddar (grated)
75ml Milk
Pinch of Salt
Pizza sauce *(see page 10)*
Mozzarella
Pizza Toppings of your Choice

Method

1. Make the dough by placing the olive oil and flour into a bowl and mix together.
2. Add the Cheddar and a little milk and mix. Continue adding the remainder of the milk a little at a time until it forms a dough.
3. Roll out the dough on a floured surface and shape into a circle of ½ cm thickness to a slightly smaller size than your air fryer basket. (You may need to cook the pizzas separately, depending on the size of your air fryer).
4. The dough is now ready for you to add the toppings of your choice.
5. Spray the air fryer basket and place the pizza inside.
6. Cook at 180°c for 10-15 minutes, checking during cooking. Once the topping and crust is golden, remove from the air fryer and serve.

See the homemade pizza sauce on page 10.

Calzone
Serves 2 (cut in half)

Ingredients
Dough
100ml warm Milk (any type)
50ml warm Water (not boiled)
1 tsp Dried Yeast
250g Strong Flour
2 tbsp Olive Oil
Pinch of Salt

Filling
4 tbsp Pizza Topping (see page 10), Tomato Ketchup or Tomato Passata
25g Cubed Cheese (Feta, Mozzarella or Cheddar Cheese)
25g Cheddar Cheese (grated)
50g Salami
6 Cherry Tomatoes
6 Basil Leaves
Pinch Mixed Dried Herbs

Method

1   In a large bowl, place the warm milk, water and dried yeast. Mix and leave for 5 minutes.
2   Add the flour and mix to form a dough. Kneed for 5 minutes or use a food mixer with a dough hook. Then kneed in the olive oil.
3   Cover the bowl with a damp tea towel and leave in a warm place to rise for 1 hour.
4   Add the salt to the dough and kneed into a large round circle to make the pizza base.
5   Spread pizza base with the pizza topping then add the cheeses, salami, tomatoes, mixed herbs and basil leaves.

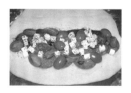

6   Brush milk around the edge of the dough circle and fold in half like a pasty.
7   Flour both sides and place on an ovenproof deep dish that is suitable for your air fryer, cook at 170°c for 15-20 minutes until golden brown and cooked through. Serve with a mixed salad.

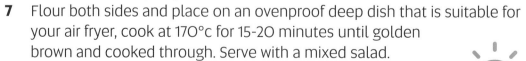

Use vegan cheese and add more vegetables instead of salami for a delicious, vegan treat.

Cod Parcel
Serves 1

Ingredients

240g Fillet of
Cod (sliced
lengthways)
25g Butter
2 slices Parma
Ham
Sprig of Parsley
(chopped)
Salt & Pepper

Method

1 Lay out the slices of Parma ham on a
board. Place the cod fillets width
ways on top.
2 Soften the butter in a small bowl,
chop the parsley and combine
together.
3 Divide the butter mixture into two
and spread some of the mixture on
top of the cod fillets. Bring up the
sides of the ham over each cod fillet
to wrap. Spread the remaining butter
mixture on top.
4 Place in an ovenproof dish suitable
for your air fryer and cook for 15
minutes at 180°c.

Serve with new potatoes and vegetables or peas.

Lime, Ginger & Chilli Salmon Fillets
Serves 2

Ingredients

2 Salmon Fillets

2 tbsp Lime Juice

1 tsp Ginger (minced)

1tsp Chilli Flakes

Spray Oil

Tin Foil

Method

1   Take 2 sheets of tin foil, spray with oil.

2   Place a salmon fillet on each piece of tin foil and add 1 tbsp lime juice, ½ tsp minced ginger, ½ tsp chilli flakes. Spray oil on top of each fillet and wrap up the foil around the salmon.

3   Place the salmon parcels into the basket of the air fryer and cook at 180°c for 8 minutes.

4   Unwrap the parcels (be careful of escaping steam) and pour the accumulated juice over salmon fillets and serve with baby potatoes and steamed vegetables.

Use the lemon and herb marinade from page 7 as an alternative dressing.

Herb Crusted Fish
Serves 2

Ingredients

2 medium White Fish Fillets (Cod, Hake, Sea Bass or similar)

4 tbsp Breadcrumbs

2 tbsp Fresh Parmesan (grated)

1 tbsp fresh Parsley (chopped)

2 tbsp Olive Oil

1 tbsp fresh Lemon juice

2 Lemon wedges (for serving)

Method

1 Mix the breadcrumbs, parmesan cheese and parsley together in a bowl. Add oil and lemon juice to make a paste.
2 Place the cod fillets on a round, lightly greased or oiled ovenproof dish or tin that is suitable for an air fryer.
3 Place the paste on top of the fish, covering evenly.
4 Cook at 170°c for 10-15 minutes.

Serve with a lemon wedge and your favourite potatoes and vegetables.

Why not use crushed tortilla chips as an alternative to breadcrumbs to make a delicious, gluten free fish dish?

Frittata 🌿

Serves 4

Ingredients

Cooking Spray
Oil
1 Red Onion
(peeled and
sliced)
2 Large Potatoes
(peeled and
cubed)
4 Large Eggs
15ml Double Cream
15ml Milk
1 tbsp Water
1 pinch Cayenne Pepper *(optional)*

Filling Choices

50g Sliced Red Pepper
50g Diced Chorizo Sausage
50g Chopped Fresh Tomato
50g Diced Ham
2 Cooked & Sliced Pork Sausages
50g Grated Cheddar

Method

1   Cook cubed potatoes in boiling water for 10 minutes and drain.
2   In a bowl, lightly whisk with a fork, the eggs, cream, milk, water and cayenne pepper *(optional)*. Season with salt & pepper.
3   Add to the egg mixture the cooked potatoes, onions and fillings of your choice.
4   Spray an ovenproof deep dish that is suitable for your air fryer with the spray oil and pour in your frittata mixture.
5   Cook at 170°c for 15-20 minutes, checking every 5 minutes until the frittata is set and lightly browned.
6   Cut into quarters and serve with a side salad.

Spice it up by adding some sliced red chilli. For a lighter, dairy free option, replace the potatoes with sweet potatoes and substitute the cream and milk for 30ml of almond milk.

Veggie Burger 🌿
Serves 6

Mains

Ingredients

1 small Onion
(finely chopped)
1 Garlic Clove
(crushed)
2 Carrots (peeled
and grated)
1 small Courgette (grated)
75g Cheese/Vegan Cheese (grated)
1 tbsp Soy Sauce
(do not use if gluten intolerant)
200g Mashed Potato
50g Sweetcorn
50g Frozen Peas
1 medium Egg/Olive Oil
200g Plain Flour/Cornflour (gf)
(plus extra for coating)
1 tbsp Olive Oil
Pinch of Mixed Herbs

Method

1 Lightly fry the onion and garlic until soft being careful not to burn them.
2 Add in the courgette, carrots, sweetcorn, frozen peas and mixed herbs, cook for a further 3 minutes.
3 Place the mashed potato in a large bowl and add in the cooked ingredients from steps 1 and 2, add the flour, soy sauce, egg and mix together.
4 Form into 6 burgers and coat in flour.
5 Chill the burgers in the fridge for an hour so that they are set ready for cooking.
6 Cook at 170°c in a lightly oiled dish suitable for an air fryer for 10 minutes on each side.
7 Serve in a burger bun with salad, onion, mayonnaise and sliced tomato.

At step 5 the burgers can be frozen and used later. Use vegan cheese and oil instead of the egg to make these suitable for vegans. By substituting the soy sauce for a pinch salt, the plain flour for cornflour and serving in a gluten free ciabatta, they are then suitable for a gluten free diet.

Vegan Stuffed Sweet Potato Skins 🌱

Ingredients
4 medium Sweet Potatoes
1 Onion (diced)
2 tsp Curry Powder
1 tsp Oil
1 tbsp Sweet Chilli Sauce
80ml Coconut Cream

Method

1   Wash and scrub the potatoes, place on a tray and cook in the air fryer at 170°c for 30 minutes. Set aside to cool. (This can be done earlier in the day or the day before and stored in a fridge).
2   In an ovenproof dish suitable for the air fryer, place the onions, oil and curry powder and cook at 180°c for 5 minutes or until soft.
3   Cut the sweet potatoes in half and scoop out the middle, and place into a bowl. Save the skins for the filling.
4   Add the cooked onion mix, sweet chilli sauce and coconut cream to the potatoes and mix together.
5   Fill the skins with your potato mixture.
6   Place potatoes into a suitable dish for air fryer and cook at 170°c for 10-15 minutes.

Add some grated vegan cheese on top of potatoes at stage 5 for a crispy cheesy topping.

Vegan Cauliflower Steaks 🌱

Serves 2

Ingredients

1 Head of
Cauliflower
1 tbsp Oil
1 tbsp Lemon Juice
¼ tsp Salt

Add some Flavour

1 Garlic Clove (finely chopped)
1 tsp Medium Curry Power
1 tsp Chilli Powder

Method

1 Wash the cauliflower head and cut into 1 inch steaks leaving the core intact.
2 In a bowl, mix your chosen flavour with the oil, lemon juice and salt. Spread onto both sides of the steak and marinate for 1 hour.
3 Place in the air fryer in single layers (may need to cook in batches) and cook at 170°c for 15 minutes, checking every 5 minutes and turning half way through.
4 Serve with quinoa, boiled rice or potatoes of your choice.

Serve with vegan mayonnaise mixed with with 1 tsp lemon and ½ clove of chopped garlic.

Vegan Meat Loaf 🌱
Serves 4

Ingredients

125g Mushrooms (sliced)
50g Plain Cashew Nuts
100g Plain Mixed Nuts
75g Quinoa
90g Dried Bulgur Wheat
1 Vegetable Stock Cube with 500ml boiling water
2 slices of Vegan Bread (breadcrumbs)
100g Plain Flour
2 small Onions (finely chopped)
1 Sweet Potato (peeled & finely diced)
50g Vegan Margarine or 3 tbsp Oil
4 Garlic Cloves (finely chopped)
1 tsp Mixed Herbs
2 tbsp Cranberry Sauce
Pinch Salt & Pepper

Method

1 In a suitable ovenproof dish for your air fryer, fry the onion with 40g margarine or 2 tbsp of oil for 2 minutes at 170°c.
2 Add the mushrooms and cook for a further 2 minutes.
3 Add the garlic, quinoa, bulgur wheat and cook another 2 minutes.
4 Add the stock (stock cube mixed with 500ml of boiling water) and cranberry sauce.
5 Season, stir cover with tin foil and cook for 10 minutes.
6 Add the sweet potato and cook for 5 minutes.
7 In a bowl, mix together the flour, nuts and breadcrumbs. Add this to the other ingredients and stir together.
8 Pour mixture into a greased ovenproof deep dish/loaf tin that is suitable for your air fryer. Add 10g margarine or 1 tbsp of oil and 2 tbsp water on top and cook in the air fryer at 170°c for 10-15 minutes, checking every 5 minutes until cooked.

Make gluten free by changing the bread to gluten free bread. Make quick breadcrumbs by tearing up your bread, placing in a food processor and pulse until finely crumbed. (Stale Bread works best).

Desserts

Puff Pastry Apple Roses

Makes 6

Ingredients

2 Red Apples, thinly sliced
50g Sultanas
160g Ready Rolled Puff Pastry
2 tbsp Apricot Jam
2 tbsp Water
1 tsp Ground Cinnamon
1 tbsp Lemon Juice
50g Butter
2 tsp Brown Sugar

Method

1. Core and thinly slice the apple, add to a bowl and cover with water. Add the lemon juice and cover with cling film, cook in microwave at full power for 2-3 minutes, until the apples are soft.
2. Unroll the pastry and cut width-ways into 6 equal parts.
3. In a bowl, mix together the jam with 2 tbsp water.
4. Working with one strip at a time, coat the pastry strip with the jam mixture. Arrange the apple slices length-ways on the top half of the pastry with the skin at the top. Sprinkle a few sultanas along pastry and then a small amount of cinnamon. *(See picture)*.

5. Fold the pastry over to cover the bottom of the apple slices. Coat the top of the pastry with melted butter. Roll the Strip from one end to the other to create a rose.
6. Place the rose in a silicone cup case or ramekin and repeat until all 6 are done.
7. Brush the tops of the apple with the remaining melted butter and sprinkle with brown sugar.
8. Loosely cover the cases with tin foil.
9. Place the silicone cases into the air fryer basket (may need be done in batches depending on the size of the air fryer).
10. Cook at 170°c for 10 minutes, uncover and cook for a further 5-10 minutes until golden brown.
11. Allow to cool and remove from cases. Serve warm with whipped cream or ice cream.

Banana Cake
Serves 6

Ingredients

150g Self Raising Flour
150g Butter (room temperature)
150g Caster Sugar
3 Large Eggs
2 Soft Bananas (peeled & mashed)
1 tsp Vanilla Essence
1 tsp Cinnamon

Method

1. Mix the flour, butter, sugar, egg, cinnamon and vanilla essence together in a bowl.
2. Add the banana to the mixture and stir.
3. Grease a loaf tin or similar that is suitable for an air fryer and pour in the cake mixture.
4. Cook at 170°c for 30-35 minutes, until a knife comes out clean from the centre of the cake.

Use an over ripe (brown) banana for a more intense flavour. You could add a handful of mixed fruit into step 1 with the flour if desired.

Lemon and Poppy Seed Muffins

Makes 6

Ingredients

75ml Vegetable Oil or softened Butter
75ml Milk
100g Caster Sugar
1 Egg
150g Self Raising Flour
Pinch Salt
½ tsp Vanilla Essence
2 Lemons (juiced and the zest of 1)
10g Poppy Seeds
6 Muffin cases

Method

1   Put the vegetable oil/butter, milk, sugar, egg, flour, salt and vanilla essence in a bowl and mix.
2   Carefully fold in the lemon juice, zest and the poppy seeds.
3   Place 6 muffin cases into silicone cases or ramekins.
4   Divide the muffin mixture between the cases and place them into the air fryer.
5   Bake at 170°c for 20-25 minutes until a knife comes out clean from the centre of the muffins.
6   Allow to cool and serve.

Depending on the size of your air fryer, you may have to cook in 2 separate batches.

Use 200g of your favourite fruit or 100g chocolate chips instead of the lemon and poppy seeds for a more indulgent muffin.

Oaty Fruit Crumble

Desserts

Ingredients

Crumble Topping
225g Plain Flour
110g Butter (cold)
110g Sugar
100g Oats

Filling
700g chosen Fruit (peeled, cored, de-seeded and chopped)
60g Butter (melted)
2 tsp Lemon Juice (if using apples)
25g White or Brown sugar (to taste depending on the sweetness of the fruit)

Method

1. Place flour and sugar in a bowl, grate in the cold butter and rub in between your fingers until the mixture is a fine breadcrumb consistency.
2. Mix in the oats to the crumble topping.
3. Place the fruit in an ovenproof dish that is suitable for an air fryer.
4. Pour the pre-melted butter over the fruit and sprinkle on the sugar. If you are using hard fruits (apples, pear or rhubarb) cook for 10-15 minutes at 170°c before the next step.
5. Evenly sprinkle the crumble mixture over the fruit, do not press it down.
6. Bake at 170°c for 30-40 minutes until golden brown.

Optional extras: You can add to the basic crumble mix, 50g chopped walnuts or mixed nuts (to make it extra crunchy).

Why not add some dried fruit into your base for an extra twist?

Chocolate Cherry Brownie

Serves 8

Ingredients

200g Plain Chocolate
155g Butter
3 Eggs
100g Muscovado Sugar
50g Cocoa Powder
75g Plain Flour
100g Glace Cherries

Method

1 Break up the chocolate in a bowl and add butter. Melt in microwave for 1-2 minutes, stirring every 30 seconds until smooth. Cook longer if required.
2 Grease an ovenproof deep dish that is suitable for your air fryer.
3 Whisk the eggs and sugar together in bowl. Add cocoa powder and the melted chocolate to mixture and stir. Fold in the plain flour and cherries.
4 Place brownie mixture into the greased ovenproof dish.
5 Cook at 170°c for 10-15 minutes, checking every 5 minutes. Cooking times will vary depending on the gooeyness preferred.
6 Allow to slightly cool and carefully remove from dish.
7 Cut into 8 portions and serve with ice cream or whipped cream.

Use black cherries soaked with Kirsch instead of glace cherries for an extra delight.
Add extra naughtiness by adding 50g of white chocolate chips to step 3.

Chocolate Chip Cookie Cake
Serves 6

Desserts

Ingredients

50g Butter
50g Brown Sugar
1 Egg
100g Plain Flour
½ tsp Baking Powder
½ tsp Baking Soda
1 tbsp Golden Syrup
1 tsp Vanilla Essence
100g Chocolate Chips
50g Sultanas (*optional*)

Method

1 Grease an ovenproof deep dish that is suitable for your air fryer.
2 Cream the butter and brown sugar in a mixing bowl. Add egg and stir. Sift in flour, baking powder and baking soda, mix together. Add in the golden syrup and vanilla essence, and mix. Then fold in the chocolate chips and sultanas.
3 Transfer mixture to the greased ovenproof dish and place in air fryer.
4 Cook at 170°c for 15-20 minutes, checking every 5 minutes until golden brown.
5 Carefully remove cake from dish.

Serve warm with whipped cream or leave to cool and decorate as a birthday cookie.

For a nutty flavour, add in 100g of crushed nuts.

Hot Cross Bun Bread and Butter Pudding
Serves 2-4

Ingredients

4 Hot Cross Buns or 5 slices of Panettone
15g Butter
30g Currants or Mixed Fruit
40ml Double Cream
140ml Whole Milk
55g Caster Sugar
2 Eggs
30g Soft Brown Sugar
Grated Nutmeg to taste

Method

1   Lightly butter a suitable ovenproof deep dish that fits into your air fryer.
2   Butter all the slices of Panettone and cut them into triangles or cut the hot cross buns in half, butter and cut into triangles.
3   Cover the bottom of the dish with one third the panettone/hot cross buns and sprinkle half the fruit and caster sugar over the top.
4   Make another layer of panettone/hot cross bun, fruit and caster sugar as in step 3.
5   Use the last of the panettone/hot cross bun to cover the top.
6   In a large bowl, whisk together the milk, eggs and cream.
7   Pour this mixture over the bread and fruit layers and allow to soak in.
8   Finally sprinkle the brown sugar and grated nutmeg over the top.
9   Place in air fryer at 170°c for 25-35 minutes until the top is golden and crunchy.

Add 50ml shot of Amaretto to step 6 for an extra indulgence!

If panettone or hot cross buns are unavailable replace with fruit loaf or white bread.

Alternatively finish with orange zest and serve with thick cream or ice cream.

Chocolate Croissant Pudding: Use 4 croissants instead of hot cross buns and remove the fruit and add 30g chocolate chips. Butter the croissants and then spread with a chocolate spread. Add 50g of cocoa powder into the custard mix (step 6).

Chocolate Cup Cakes
Makes 6 cupcakes

Ingredients

75g Self Raising Flour
75g Softened Butter or Margarine
1 Large Egg
75g Caster Sugar
20ml Milk
20g Cocoa Powder
½ tsp Vanilla Essence

Frosting

250g Icing Sugar
95g Butter (room temp)
40g Cocoa Powder
20ml Milk
1 tsp Gravy Browning (optional)
6 Glace Cherries or Chocolate Strands (*optional*)

Method

1   Sift the flour into a bowl and add the butter, eggs, sugar, cocoa powder, milk and vanilla essence in a bowl and mix until smooth.
2   Divide into 6 cupcake cases, place in silicone cupcake cases or ramekins and place into the air fryer.
3   Bake in the air fryer at 170°c for 15 - 20 minutes or until a knife comes out clean from the centre of the cake. Allow to cool.
4   While the cakes are cooling, make the frosting. Mix together icing sugar, butter, milk, cocoa powder, gravy browning, whisking until smooth.
5   Pipe or spoon the frosting on top of each cupcake and decorate with cherry or chocolate strands.

You will need 6 Silicone cup cake cases with paper insert (if silicone cases are not available use a ramekin that is a suitable size for use as a cupcake case)

If you have a larger air fryer ,double the ingredients for 12 cupcakes.

Flavour Variations: Add in 25g of chopped glace cherries, 25g chocolate chips or 25g desiccated coconut for an extra indulgence.
Gluten free: Replace the flour for cornflour or corn starch.
Dairy Free: Replace the butter for a dairy free/vegan margarine.

Coconut & Jam Cookies
12 Cookies

Ingredients

125g Butter
75g Light Brown Sugar
1 Egg (yolk & white separated)
½ tsp Mixed Spice
80g Plain Flour
80g Ground Almonds
Zest of 1 Lemon
2 tbsp Raspberry Jam
5 tbsp Desiccated Coconut

Method

1 In a bowl, mix together the butter, brown sugar and lemon zest. Add in the egg yolk and stir. Slowly add in the flour, ground almonds and mixed spice to make a dough.

2 In a separate bowl, lightly beat the egg white until frothy. In a separate bowl then place the desiccated coconut.

3 Roll the dough into 12 small balls, then coat the balls in the egg white and then in the coconut.

4 Place each ball in a silicone cupcake case or a ramekin.

5 Make an imprint in the middle of each ball with your thumb or the end of a wooden spoon and fill with jam.

6 Place the silicone cupcake cases into the air fryer (may need to be cooked in two batches, depending on the size of your air fryer).

7 Cook at 170°c for 15-20 minutes or until golden brown.
Check every 5 minutes whilst cooking.

You will need 6 Silicone cup cake cases with paper insert (if silicone cases are not available use a ramekin that is a suitable size for use as a cupcake case).
Make gluten free by replacing the flour with cornflour.
Use your favourite jam or chocolate instead of raspberry jam.

Almond Mince Pies

Makes 6

Ingredients
Almond
Pastry

110g Plain Flour

25g Ground Almonds

100g Cold Butter (cut into cubes)

A little Cold Water

35g Caster Sugar

Pinch Salt

Mince Pie Filling

75g Sultanas

75g Raisins

75g Mixed Dried Fruit

30g Glace Cherries (halved)

1 tbsp Cherry Brandy

1 tbsp Port

25g Brown Sugar

10g Butter

10g Mixed Peel

Method

1 **Almond Pastry:** in a bowl place the flour, ground almonds, sugar and salt. Add in the butter cubes and rub with fingers to form a breadcrumb consistency. Slowly add in a small amount of cold water to form a dough.

2 Wrap the dough in cling film and allow dough to rest in the fridge for 30 minutes.

3 **Mince Pie Filling:** In an ovenproof dish that is suitable for the air fryer, place the mince pie filling ingredients and mix. Cook at 170°c for 5-10 minutes. Allow to cool.

4 Roll out the pastry to approx. 5mm thickness, use a pastry cutter to cut circles to fit as a base in a cupcake case or ramekin.

5 Place the tart bases into 6 silicone cupcake cases or ramekins.

6 Place a spoonful of filling in each of the pastry bases.

7 For the pie tops, cut the left-over pastry into strips and place on top of pie in a lattice pattern.

8 Brush the pie tops with milk or beaten egg.

9 Place silicone cases into the air fryer and cook at 170°c for 15-20 minutes. Checking every 5 minutes.

10 Once cooked, allow to cool and remove from silicone cases. Sprinkle with icing sugar and serve with a dollop of whipped cream.

Measurement Guide
(rough guide)

Tsp : Teaspoon

Tbsp: Tablespoon

G: Grams

Lb: Pound

Pt: Pint

Fl oz: Fluid Ounce

Oz: Ounce

Ml: Millilitre

Lt: Litre

Dried Ingredients

5ml: 1 teaspoon

25g or 1 oz: 1 heaped tablespoon

50g = 1.7 oz

75g = 2.64 oz

100g = 3.5 oz

450g = 15.8oz = 1 lb

Wet Ingredients:

125ml = ¼ pt = 4.3fl oz

250ml = ½ pt = 8.4fl oz

500ml = 1 pt = 17fl oz

1lt = 2 pts = 35fl oz

Measurements:

1cm = 0.39 inches

2.4cm = 1 inches

15cm = 5.9 inches

Oven Temperature:

150°c = Gas Mark 2 = 300°f

160°c = Gas Mark 2.5 = 315°f

170°c = Gas Mark 3 = 325°f

180°c = Gas Mark 4 = 350°f

190°c = Gas Mark 5 = 375°f

200°c = Gas Mark 6 = 400°f

220°c = Gas Mark 7 = 425°f

INDEX